CENZONTLE/ MOCKINGBIRD

Songs of Empowerment
(Poetry * Drama)

YA Edition

by Daniel García Ordaz

CENZONTLE/ MOCKINGBIRD

Songs of Empowerment

(Poetry * Drama)

YA Edition

by Daniel García Ordaz

El Zarape Press
McAllen, Texas

Published by El Zarape Press Press: McAllen TX USA

Cenzontle/Mockingbird: Songs of Empowerment
(Poetry * Drama) YA Edition
Poetry—American. Poetry—World. Poetry—Young Adult.
Poetry—Mexican American.
Poetry—Collection.

ISBN-13: 978-1-7328106-0-0
ISBN-10: 1-7328106-0-5

Cover artwork designed by Gabriel Martínez
Printed in the United States of America.

DEDICATION

To Maya Angelou and Gloria E. Anzaldúa, and to Langston Hughes and Pablo Neruda, to Lorca and Whitman and Lazarus and Frost and Dickens and Dickinson. To Roberto Gómez Bolaños (Chespirito) and Eduardo Manzano y Enrique Cuenca (Los Polivoces.) Your words linger in me as I loiter in yours. To Lloyd Alexander for being my home base. To Walter Wangerin, Jr. for helping me see the possibilities.

To Mom and Dad's grandkids, Joshua, Laura, Anna, and Steven, Charlie, Ximene, Mace Deon, Marissa, Marco Jr., Karel, Art Jr., Marcus, Monica, Erika, Rita, Joseph, Theodore, and Felix Jr.

To my grandmothers, mi Abuelita Fina and mi Abuelita Chuy, whose voices still sing in my heart. To my wife, Gina, and our nieces Payton and McKenna. To my late father, Macedonio García, Sr., my mom, Rosa María Ordaz vda. de García, and my brothers and sisters. Of thee I sing.

To my students, past and present: May you be inspired. Thank you for inspiring and teaching me.

To Jen Mendoza, Michael Jones, and Gina M. García for helping me write some questions contained herein.

To Edward Vidaurre and Rene Saldaña, Jr., for encouraging a Young Adult edition of my book.

To Gabriel Martínez, the cover artist, for working with me patiently as we toiled through several changes.

To my fellow teachers and educators for your mentorship and friendship, especially David Moore, Rachelle Downey, Luis Garza, Sam Moreno, Joe and Wendy Ramos, John Flores, and fellow educators at La Joya Early College, McHi, Weslaco East, IDEA, and McAllen Memorial High School.

To librarians, for your love of and dedication to books and writers and readers and for your support: Adolfo García, Armandina Sesin, Arnold Becho, Brenda Huston, Catherine Salinas, Elizabeth Hollenbeck, José Tamez, Josie Cornejo, Letty Leija, Lolly Peña, Lou Sarabando, Lupita Nava, Margie Longoria, Noe Torres, Norma Garza, Norma Gomez Fultz, and Renee Dyer.

CONTENTS

ACKNOWLEDGEMENTS

Grateful acknowledgement to the editors of the following journals and publications, where some of the following works have appeared:

Praxis Magazine Online: "Cenzontle"

Juventud! Growing up on the Border (VAO Publishing): "La Labor: Migrantes del Valle"

Poetry of Resistance: Voices For Social Justice (The University of Arizona Press): "Immigrant Crossing"

La Bloga Online Floricanto: "Our Serpent Tongue," "Immigrant Crossing," and "Oda de Odiseo a la Sirena"

Left Hand of the Father: "My Dearest Nadine"

Harbinger Asylum: "In-A-God, A-New-Vita"

Interstice: "La Toronja," "Numbered Days," "En La Pulga," and "Creation"

Encore: Cultural Arts Source: "Frida y Sus Sueños"

100 Thousand Poets For Change: "*In America*"

Gallery: A Literary & Arts Magazine (UTRGV): "Romeo & Juliet ¿Y Qué?"

Texas Intercollegiate Press Association: 3rd Place: Spanish Story: "Romeo & Juliet ¿Y Qué?"

Caja de Resistencia: "Immigrant Crossing"

Resist Much/Obey Little: Inaugural Poems to the Resistance (Spuyten Duyvil Publishing): "Immigrant Crossing"

* * *

I would also acknowledge those who've awarded my writing or included me as a guest or panelist or featured poet or keynote speaker at countless schools, libraries, organizations, and festivals.

Border Book Bash
Dallas International Book Fair
FESTIBA
Gemini Ink Writers Conference
McAllen Book Festival
South Texas College
Texas Association for the Improvement of Reading
Texas Associated Press Managing Editors
Texas Association of Bilingual Educators
Texas Book Festival
Texas Center For The Book
Texas Intercollegiate Press Association
Texas Library Association
University of the Incarnate Word
University of Texas Rio Grande Valley

AUTHOR'S PREFACE

Cenzontle/Mockingbird: Poetry As Empowerment

This book contains questions and writing prompts. I hope they will add to your reading and performative and educational experience.

They say that in order to understand someone, you must walk a mile in their shoes. The contents herein are meant just for that purpose—except instead of shoes, these are other people's voices—and by performing them, I hope we all get to know one another a little better. The poems, monologues, and play adaptation here are meant to be performed. They are polyglossic and polysemous. Like a mockingbird, whom the Aztecs call "cenzontle" in their Nahuatl tongue, my writer's voice is polyvoiced. I include in this collection an eclectic variety of voices: personas, languages, forms, styles, and identities—often mixing them, in part to entertain and in part to challenge my boundaries as a writer, to stretch my vocal chords, so to speak, but also in part to challenge the lingering prejudice against such *mestizaje*—or meeting and mixing of cultures (and also voices)—and help convert our society into one that accepts itself as it is: polyglossic and stronger for it. As Maya Angelou reminded us, indeed "We are more alike, my friends, than we are unalike." The sooner we embrace that truth, the sooner we can all join in the song that is America—the song that includes blues and jazz and *conjunto* and zydeco and yodeling and rap and bluegrass twang and *zapateadas*.

I approached the writing and the collecting, in part, as social criticism—as a necessary response to those prejudices that often pervade our attitudes around language and underlie interactions between and among the dominant class and Latinx, Hispanics, Chicanx, women, and other minority groups. I say "among" as well as "between" because some biases often pit, for example, Latino versus Latino—usually based on socio-economic status (evidenced by use of language and not by economic markers).

Ultimately, I wish for readers to acknowledge first that despite the recent evolution towards more welcoming attitudes regarding diversity in general and multilingualism in particular, writing in the U.S. is still generally expected to be produced in Standard American English. I wish for readers to acknowledge that I (and many like me) already appreciate and embrace texts by English-speaking writers of varying styles and voices; we simply seek some reciprocity. My collection is yet another invitation toward acceptance of linguistic diversity.

I use mimicry—in the kindest sense of the word—as a form of empowerment, not to crash the American party with an appetite for destruction, but for the sake of creating unity by celebrating the richness of American voices. Likewise, I invite the reader to mimic my work as tool of empowerment towards unity. My mentor and friend, Dr. Debbie Cole, a linguistic anthropologist, argues in her doctoral dissertation that performing "articulations of 'unity' using the familiar sounds of linguistic diversity enables ideological change . . . ." That is, "we can commit to recognizing diversity by sounding others' voices with our voices." In that vein, it is my sincere hope that the reader will recognize his or her voice in my writings and that the reader will "sound" my literary voice so that we may all be empowered to create unity through our diversity.

For the male mockingbird, the ultimate goal is not to mock or mimic or even to show off. The ultimate goal in his sounding off in diverse voices is to gain a mate—to attract a female with whom to unite and procreate. America has more than one voice and more than one song. Let's sing together!

Lift Every Voice and Sing

"Words mean more than what is set down on paper. It takes the human voice to infuse them with shades of deeper meaning."
~ Maya Angelou

Cenzontle*
(For Maya Angelou)

"Mockingbirds don't do one thing but make music for us to enjoy . . . but sing their hearts out for us. That's why it's a sin to kill a mockingbird."

~Harper Lee, To Kill a Mockingbird

And what makes a mockingbird special, anyway?
Why it's the trill from her tongue,
the cry from her lungs,
the sway of her lips,
it's her dusty, rusty, crusty cries,
the trail of tears in her eyes
on sheet music playin',
floatin' and swayin'
to the beat, beat, beating, way-laying,
saxopholaying,
assaulted, accosted, bushwhacked and busted,
cracked open, bruised, banged and accused,
flat broke and broken terror bespoken –
a token of survivin',
of thrivin', of juke joint jump jivin'
of death cheaten daily through unwanton wailin'.

Why a mockingbird's got diamonds
at the souls of her blues,
whip-lashed back-beats
at the edge of her grooves,
croons of healing above strangely-fruited plains of grieving.
She lets loose veracity with chirps
still rising at the edge of a knockabout life,
troubled and toiled
beat-boxed, embroiled,
de-plumed, defaced, ignored, encased,

caged and debased 'cause of the color of her skin.
But as the din fades and the cool of eve rolls in,
there she stands—chest huff-puffed and proud,
unbowed and loud, endowed
with the power of flight,
under the big dip of night,
echoing the ancient *Even* cry of a lioness
defending her pride
in that sweet mother tongue:

> I rise up, and, *Adam*,
> I shall not be moved today!

The mockingbird sings what the heart cannot pray.
The mockingbird sings what the heart cannot pray.

*Cenzontle is the Nahuatl word for the northern mockingbird, *Mimus polyglottos*.

QUESTIONS

1. What is significant about the poem beginning with the word "and"?
2. What figures of speech do you experience in the poem?
3. What allusions do you recognize in the poem?
4. What tones are detected in the poem?
5. Would this poem succeed as a monologue?
6. How does the poet use gender to reveal the theme of the poem?
7. Who is the mockingbird? How does the title fit the poem?
8. What is empowering about this poem?

To the Poets, To Make Much of Rhyme

You say you're a poet
'Cause you know
How to rhyme
All the time
Pantomime
Share your mind
Hit the stage
Show your rage
Be a sage
Despite your young age.

He will tell you to
Stop it!
when you
Emulate Neruda's style,
Walk a mile in Frost-ed flakes,
Shape your quips with Maya's guile,
Light a little dream of Langston's fuse,
Yaup with Whitman for a while,
Paint your muse in blue Plath hues.

He'll ask,
Who are you to be a poet?
As if poetry must be licensed and controlled.
He'll say,
Poetry is a luxury.
As if poetry is made of white-hot platinum gold.
A commodity of high society.
Untouchable.
Unteachable.
Unreachable.

But the fact remains that poetry is only for the bold.
To be a poet is to share truth.

To withhold knowledge is for the brute.
To be a poet is to be a conscious voice—
To rise above the pleasant noise.

We pledge allegiance to the math and science in order to survive.
But if we really want to be alive—to thrive—
We must learn to dive into the deep end of the pool—
Leave behind the idea of being cool:
Embrace shame!   failure!   fear!
Run naked on the street.
Play with words that refuse to let us sleep.
Mold our words with passion and desire.
Dare to write as if our heart's on fire . . . .

So when he asks,
Who are you to be a poet?
I say,
Who is he to even ask?
You're the one who stepped up boldly to the mic.
He's the one still sitting with his class.

QUESTIONS

1. The speaker is addressing poets or would-be poets, but who is "He"?
2. How does the speaker describe the role of the poet?
3. How would you describe the writer's craft, based on the poem?
4. How would you describe the author's use of rhyme?
5. What figures of speech do you experience in the poem?
6. What allusions do you recognize in the poem?
7. What is the speaker's overall tone?
8. What is empowering about this poem?

A Las Lenguas, Que Sigan Sus Cantos

A veces le decimos adiós a nuestro language.
En vez de tacos en la calle
Nos fijamos a ver que hay en el re-fridge.
No se si entre este río
Habrá un suficiente land bridge
Para conectar los dos lados
De nuestra cultural heritage
Y a nuestros hijos poder cantarles
El viejo message
En el lenguaje salvaje
De nuestro mestizaje.

¡Qué viva México!
¡Qué viva México!

Que aunque suba nuestro American aprendizaje,
Que el México en nosotros no se baje.
Quédense, lenguas, calientitas
Como el té de canela
De nuestras abuelitas,
Como el caldo tlalpeño
De nuestras madrecitas.
Y no se pongan, lenguas, tibias.
Sigan cantando el viejo mensaje
En el lenguaje salvaje
De nuestro mestizaje.

¡Qué viva México!
¡Qué viva México!

¡Quita de tus platos ese sándwich!
Y enséñate a comer el viejo language!

Our Serpent Tongue
(For Gloria E. Anzaldúa)

Your Pedro Infantecide stops here.
There shall be no mending of the fence.

You set this bridge called my back
yard ablaze with partition, division
labelization, fronterization
y otras pendejadas de
alienization

Yo soy Tejan@
Mexico-American@
Chican@ Jodid@
Pagan@-Christian@

Pelad@ Fregad@

I flick the slit
at the tip of my tongue
con orgullo

knowing

que when a fork drops, es que ¡Ahí viene visita!

a woman is coming
a woman with cunning
a woman sin hombre with a forked tongue is running
her mouth—¡hocicona!—
a serpent-tongued ¡fregona! with linguistic cunning
a cunning linguist

turning her broken token of your colonization
into healing

y pa' decir la verdad

You are not my equal
You cannot speak like me
You will not speak for me

My dreams are not your dreams
My voice is not your voice

You yell, "Oh, dear Lord!"
in your dreams.
I scream "A la Fregada!"
in my nightmares

Your Pedro Infantecide stops here.
There shall be no mending of the fence.

QUESTIONS for "A Las Lenguas, Que Sigan Sus Cantos" and "Our Serpent Tongue"

1. The poet, editor, and publisher all decided not to italicize non-Standard American English words to what effect?
2. In either poem, the speaker stands in defense of what?
3. How would you describe the intended audience for each poem?
4. What is the connection to Gloria E. Anzaldúa in either poem?
5. What is empowering about these selections?

WRITING PROMPTS

1. Write a composition to a family member, teacher, or perhaps classmates expressing your wish to preserve something sacred.
2. Write a rant addressing something you feel strongly about.

Songs of (In A Sense) An Experience

"A bird doesn't sing because it has an answer. It sings because it has a song."
~ Maya Angelou

Famous

Has anyone seen my lost fifteen minutes of fame?
See, I just set them down for a minute
And things just ain't seem the same.

Okay I know that sounds kind of lame

But, naw, see, I was famous once, yo!
Shoot, I was like the next biggest thing
On YouTube.
For, like   almost a whole week!

Man, I have done it all for the camera!
I've smoked ten cigarettes through each nostril in my nose and
I went water skiing on the lake the other day without my clothes
and
Last week I ran through the mall with my momma's panty hose
Around my face.
I even had my boy spray me with Mace!

On purpose.

While the cameras were rolling.

See, if you really wanna be famous
that's just the kind of sacrifice you're gonna have to make.
'Cause when you're surfing on top of a van goin' like 30 miles-per-hour
You'd better believe
You only get one take.

That's how I broke two ribs and got this limp.
People be, like,
"Dude, did you really break your legs
Or're you just walkin' like a pimp?"

But, nah, I'll be a'ight.
I'm just waiting for Hollywood to call.
Naw, seriously though.
Naw, for real, I'm fixin' to have it all, y'all!
Cars and money and things and . . . stuff.

I'm talkin' 'bout movie roles and real expensive clothes,
And my own mansion filled with Hostess Cupcakes.
Shoot, I'm 'a have my own island on my own sea
You know, just until they name a planet after me.

'Cause as long as the camera's rolling live and on the air
I'll do anything that most people wouldn't dare,
I'll be so famous people have to stop and stare.
Talkin' 'bout, "Dang! That dude's so famous it ain't even
    fair!"
Man, I'll be livin' larger than a Grizzly bear! (Grrr)
I can break every rule and the cops don't even care.
I'll have a posse of bodyguards around with four or five to
    spare.
I'll even have a different girlfriend every morning with two
big breakfastses to share

Shoot, I'ma have my very own designer underwear
And my own brand of jeans.
And five television screens
in each bathroom.
So I can watch the news.
'Cause I-I can't read.

But, you know, at least I'll be "famous."

* * *

If you really want to be the star of your generation
Put the camera down,
And get yourself a college education.

QUESTIONS

1. What role does the speaker's bravado play in characterization?
2. How does the author use humor to relate the theme of the poem?
3. How would you describe the author's use of rhyme?
4. What figures of speech do you experience in the poem?
5. Describe the syntactical device the author uses to broadcast the shift.
6. Would this poem succeed as a theatrical monologue?
7. Is hoping for fame a generational longing or an unspoken wish?
8. This section, Songs of (In A Sense) An Experience, deals with innocence and experience—a play on words alluding to William Blake's late 18th Century works. Is the speaker ultimately innocent or experienced?
9. What is empowering about this poem?

WRITING PROMPTS

1. Write a satirical piece (script, monologue, poem, etc.) on fame.
2. Write an essay (or make a video) on why you wish to be famous, how you will achieve fame, and what you will do with your status.

Unforbitten Love

I never dreamed that I'd be kissing you.
Star-crossed lovers often never meet.
Alas, I know that's why our love was blue.

The Fates told Cupid I was overdue.
I placed the Golden Apple at your feet.
I never dreamed that I'd be kissing you.

The bell struck twelve. I never found your shoe.
I stared at stairs and my heart lost a beat.
Alas, I know that's why our love was blue.

Love at first bite did change my point of view.
True love's first taste, they say, is bloody sweet.
I never dreamed that I'd be kissing you.

In Paradise our love was bare and true.
You let me taste your fruit that brought the heat.
Alas, I know that's why our love was blue.

My tresses locked the secret that I kept.
Your loving beauty cut them as I slept.
I never dreamed that I'd be kissing you.
Alas, I know that's why our love was blue.

QUESTIONS

1. Describe the characteristics of a villanelle, such as this and the next.
2. What allusions do you recognize in this and the next poem?
3. What is the likely gender of the multiple speakers in either poem?

Love Forbitten

I always dreamed that I'd be kissing you.
I begged for Night to come and bring my meat.
I'll never know just why our love turned blue.

I launched a-thousand ships as our love grew.
The horse, my groom, (our doom) the Fates did mete.
I always dreamed that I'd be kissing you.

The bell struck twelve. I'd hoped you'd found my shoe.
The heart of man is easy to defeat.
I'll never know just why our love turned blue.

Life's blood's a sweet bouquet when stakes are few.
In love, entombed in darkness, death we cheat.
I always dreamed that I'd be kissing you.

When Eden's serpent truth with lies imbued,
The blame you laid, like thorns, upon my feet.
I'll never know just why our love turned blue.

My beauty learned the secret that you fibbed.
You tore asunder pillars as you lived.
I always dreamed that I'd be kissing you.
I'll never know just why our love turned blue.

QUESTIONS

1. How are these two villanelles connected?
2. Who (specifically) are the speakers in the corresponding stanzas?
3. Discuss archetype, motif, and theme.
4. What is empowering about these two poems?

Frida y Sus Sueños

The bus driver got lost and arrived instead at a place in ruins
somewhere in México – surreal México.
The México that exists in dreams?
~Julieta Corpus

The bus driver got lost and arrived
Arrived instead at a place
A place in ruins
A place somewhere in México—surreal México,
The México that exists
In dreams.

In dreams about masks and death
Deathly ill Frida and her changos
Changos with sunflowers and blue skies
Blue skies bloodied with red parrots.

Red parrots attacking your skin
Your skin peeling away like molten lava
Molten lava swallowing the moon
The moon shining on skulls on murals.

The bus driver got lost and arrived
Arrived instead at a place
A place in dreams about masks and death
Deathly ill Frida and her changos

Her changos attacking your skin
Your skin peeling away like molten lava
Molten lava that exists only in surreal México
Surreal México bloodied with blue skies
Blue skies and the moon shining on skulls on murals
The moon shining on skulls in dreams.

QUESTIONS

1. What is the effect of the poet's use of anaphora?
2. What non-poet writers/orators practice anaphora?
3. This poem was written after viewing a painting by Mexican painter Frida Kahlo named Girl With Death Mask; there are two versions. What's more, the poet was gifted a line (in the epigraph) from another poet's musings upon viewing the same painting. In a way, it's ekphrasis times two. What you know about ekphrastic poetry?
4. What is the effect of the speaker's use of bilingualism?
5. Since the author, borrowing from a fellow poet, italicizes the word "México" throughout, honoring the original intent of the poet whose quote he borrows, what is the effect of pronouncing the word in Spanish—as is denoted syntactically by the accent mark?
6. The speaker seems to transpose the dreams of Kahlo with the dreams or experiences of the reader. What is the effect on the reader to be suddenly thrust into this this dream scene?
7. How does the poet use juxtaposition and hyperbole to establish the tone of the poem?
8. What tools does the poet use to achieve a surrealist presentation?
9. What is empowering about innocence?
10. What is empowering about experience?
11. What is empowering about dreams?
12. What is empowering about nightmares?

WRITING PROMPTS

1. Attempt an ekphrastic writing by viewing an unknown work of visual art: a sculpture, a photograph, a painting, or film, then write about it: a response, a journal entry, a quick-write, a made-up story, a poem. Edit it until it is worthy of publication.
2. Attempt a piece of writing using anaphora. Embed it into your next speech. Embed it into your next poem. Embed into your next pretend break-up with your next pretend significant other. Repeat! Sweet!

Songs of In Her Beauty

"Love is a condition so powerful, it may be that
which pulls the stars in the firmament. It
may be that which pushes and urges the
blood in the veins. Courage: you have
to have courage to love somebody
because you risk everything –
everything."
~ Maya Angelou

She

She was like a piece of cake.

Like the last piece of cake.

Like that corner piece of cake we all claim
with our eyes, feel entitled to in our minds,
long for in our hearts—some pining and praying shyly,
some publicly sharing our intentions.
That tiny slice of heaven only one may obtain—
The one everyone assumes is spoken-for
Yet sometimes sits untaken.

She was like the winner of that last piece of cake,
Her sweetness sweetened by the victory
of the epiphany that she was not at all enough
but rather much beyond enough, that she wasn't
full of the fluff and superfluity of the frosting of beauty
but of the substance and of layers and of hidden surprises in
her heart.

QUESTIONS

1. What is the significance of the speaker's point of view?
2. Discuss the success or failure of the extended metaphor.
3. To whom does "we" and "our" allude in the third stanza?
4. What are the syntactic and thematic ramifications of the poet's use of two short stanzas to begin the poem?
5. Should the poem have ended after the second line? After the first? After just the title?
6. The poet calls outer beauty (metaphorically "the frosting of beauty") "superfluous." Should we be spending billions of dollars and trillions of seconds on outer beauty?
7. This poem, like others in this section, deals with the theme of empowerment through the recognition and embracing of inner beauty. How does this poem achieve that theme?

Beautiful Girls
(Inspired by the film "Beautiful Girls")

Beautiful Girls is hard to spell.
Beautiful Girls are hard to tell.
Beautiful Girls aren't made of flowers,
Beautiful Girls are made of powers:
They can leap into your heart with a single smile,
Strong enough to bring guys to their knees,
Make us say "God bless you," when they sneeze.

Beautiful Girls are
Your best friend, so you don't wanna risk it

Beautiful Girls are
The worst enemies to be had:
They look so good that it's hard to be mad.

Beautiful Girls are
The sugar in my coffee,
The gravy that I sop up with a biscuit,
Three big scoops of Chunky Monkey ice cream on a
chocolate-dipped waffle cone with
    whipped cream and sprinkles on top—and you don't
    have to share with your cousin!

Beautiful Girls
Can put a chink on a soldier's armor,
Can take the stink off a pig farmer.
They know how to turn on the charm.
They know how to warm up the barn.

Beautiful Girls are
The ones that said, "No way!"
The ones that got away,
The thorn at my side,

The times that I lied.
The reasons I cried.

Beautiful Girls are
The needle in my haystack,
The only reason I ever make my bed,
The curves on my guitar,
The 99 bottles of beer on the bar,
Soft rain on roses in June,
The top 27 songs on iTunes,

Beautiful Girls are
What makes a man crazy,
What keeps a man sane.

Beautiful Girls are
Staying up late, then sleeping 'til noon,
The tears from the man in the moon,
Sharing an umbrella in the rain,
The real cause of all my pain.

Beautiful Girls can
Part a busy sidewalk
Without words;
Turn noisy walkers
Into silent gawkers.

Jaw-droppin',
Eye-poppin',
Heart-stoppin',
Beautiful Girls can turn
Grackles into green jays,
Wayward weeds into bountiful bouquets,
Troublesome waters into tropical waves,
Old bald spots into new toupees,
Nightmares into holidays.

Beautiful Girls can turn
Winter snow into summer days.

Beautiful Girls
Make flatulence seem like potpourri sprays,
Turn a tiny spark into a raging blaze.

Beautiful Girls can
Turn a frown into a grin,
Make an angel turn to sin,
Make an atheist pray again,
Make you aks 'em, "How you doin'?"

Beautiful Girls can
Pay a waiter with a smile,
Make a long day's work last just a little while,
Make a cross-country trip feel like a mile.

Beautiful Girls are sure enough
To make boys and men do stupid stuff:
Beautiful Girls
Make Humpty Dumpty get off that wall
(Fat boy was just tryin' to get a little somethin', y'all)
They make Yankee Doodle ride a pony,
Make a Muslim eat bologna,
Serve protein fanatics macaroni,
Make the butchers give up meats,
Make vegetarians skip the beets,
Make boys with no rhythm move their feets.

Beautiful Girls
Can make the Devil to repent,
Cause the Pope to give up Lent,

Beautiful Girls can
Get a cop to join the mob,
Make a mobster get a job,
Make you curl up your toes,
Take a knee and then propose.

A Beautiful Girl
Will wait to have a new name and a ring
Before she gives up the one Beautiful thing
That everybody knows Beautiful Boys are really after:
The love in her heart, forever after.

QUESTIONS

1. Does beauty exist? If it does, who gets to decide what is beautiful?
2. What is the overarching tone of the poem?
3. Analyze the meter and rhyme scheme of a few favorite stanzas in the poem. How do the irregularities you note contribute to the meaning of the poem?
4. The poet juxtaposes some serious and some silly lines throughout the poem. How do such irregularities in content affect the mood?
5. What figures of speech do you experience in the poem?
6. What allusions do you recognize in the poem?
7. Would this poem succeed as a monologue?
8. What is empowering about this poem?

WRITING PROMPTS

1. Think of a beautiful girl or woman in your life. (Not someone famous.) A friend, loved one, cousin, grandma, aunt, teacher. Write a poem or note about their beauty. Send it to them.
2. Do the same for a beautiful boy or man in your life.
3. Put up a picture of someone you truly hate. Someone detestable, loathsome. Living or dead. Famous or not. Write about one beautiful thing in the picture. (Might be the person or it might be an inconsequential object in the background, etc.: a tree, the sun, a broach or pin or hat or ear or hairstyle.)

Le Finestre, or In Which My Lover Threatens To Throw Me Out The Window

If you throw me out the window
On the morning after we,
I hope you take pleasure in exfoliating hugs
because I will gladly gulp down that glassy breakfast with glee,
let it burn down my throat and churn inside my belly.

I will clamber crags and hillsides, brave the thorny hackberry guarding your bedroom,
arrive just after dinnertime—
hungry, bleeding internally, excreting
silicone, soda ash, and limestone
through sandpaper skin reflecting the luminescence
of your scorching furnace.

Just to see you again,
I would daily peregrinate on hands and knees over newly-broken bottles—
walk straight into your loving arms
and melt into your colored pane.

QUESTIONS

1. In the second line, what does "In the morning after we" mean?
2. What figures of speech do you experience in the poem?
3. Who is the speaker of the poem?
4. What is the extended metaphor? Is it effective?
5. What is empowering about this poem?

WRITING PROMPT

Take a line you overhear in the hallway, on the bus, at a store, in any crowded place, etc., and write a poem using that line.

Oda de Odiseo a la Sirena

¿Dónde estás?

Ayer te busqué,
te hallé,
te perdí.

Hoy te buscaré otra vez.

Anoche te busque en mis brazos,
tan fuera de alcance como
la bicicleta de mi niñez—
hace mucho abandonada, jamás olvidada.

Te busqué en el eterno rugir
de tus caricias marinas
sobre las rocas
de mis memorias.

Remo y remo sin cesar
hasta que el latir en mi pecho
cae triste y silencioso,
débil sobre tu ancho mar.

Anoche escuché tu canto
en los vientos del verdor,
en los aires rumorosos sobre el abismo azul
suspiros que iluminaron mi paladar
con sabor a tí.

Extraño los murmullos
que dejaste como un eco dormilón
en el hueco de mi corazón.

Me dejaste como navegante sin estrella,
vagando hacia el horizonte gris,
extraviado, aislado, abandonado.

Ayer te busqué,
te hallé,
te perdí

Hoy te buscaré otra vez
aunque sigas enviando
tus olas de besos a dioses lejanos
chocando saludos
como holas de adiós.

PREGUNTAS

1. ¿Cuál es el efecto del uso del hablante de un apóstrofo dramático?
2. ¿Qué elementos poéticos reconoces en el poema?
3. ¿Qué alusiones reconoces en el poema?
4. ¿Cómo describirías el tono del poema?
5. ¿Tendría éxito este poema como un monólogo?
6. ¿Cómo se compara este poema con el "Ulises" de Alfred, Lord Tennyson?
7. El poema fue escrito originalmente en español y traducido por el autor. ¿Qué se pierde o gana en la traducción?
8. ¿Cómo puede el lector sentirse empoderado al leer esta selección?

Ode Of Odysseus To The Siren
(a translation by Daniel García Ordaz)

Where are you?

Yesterday I sought you,
I found you
I lost you.

Today I shall seek you again.

Last night I sought you in my arms
as far from my reach as
the bicycle of my childhood—
long ago abandoned, never forgotten.

I looked for you in the eternal roar
of your marine caresses
over the rocks
of my memories.

I row and row incessantly
Until the beating in my chest
Falls sad and silent,
Debilitated over your wide sea.

Last night I heard your song
in the winds of the green,
in the gossiping airs over the blue abyss
sighs that illuminated my palate
with flavor of you.

I miss the murmurs
that you left like a sleepy echo
in the hollow of my heart.

You left me as a starless navigator,
wandering toward the gray horizon,
lost, isolated, abandoned.

Yesterday I searched for you,
I found you,
I lost you

Today I shall look for you again
even as you keep sending
waves of kisses to distant gods,
greetings crashing
like waves of hello/goodbye.

QUESTIONS

1. What is the effect of the speaker's use of dramatic apostrophe?
2. What poetic elements do you recognize in the poem?
3. What allusions do you recognize in the poem?
4. How would you describe the tone of the poem?
5. Would this poem succeed as a monologue?
6. How does this poem compare to Alfred, Lord Tennyson's "Ulysses"?
7. The poem was originally written in Spanish and translated by the author. What is lost or gained in translation?
8. What is empowering about this selection?

Grapefruit Triptych

La Toronja

The flirtatious grapefruit
Blushes, ripe and round.
Wedged inside,
Her pink flesh hides
A bitter veil.

Her yellow shell,
Now broken,
Reveals white underpants.
Her daughters, desperate to be set free,
Escape into an ocean of sour waves.

La Toronja Japonesa

Flirtacious grapefruit.
Blushing yellow rind. Bitter
veil hides pink flesh.

La Toronja Hay(na)küensa

flirtatious
grapefruit blushing
behind white veil

QUESTIONS

1. What is the structural difference between a haiku and a hay(na)ku?
2. Each subsequent version of this poem is reduced. How does this achieve one of the characteristics of poetry? Is anything lost in the reduction?

Songs of Merriment and Exaltation

"In the struggle lies the joy."
~Maya Angelou

En La Pulga

"Quiero que me entierren/en Wal-Mart.
Es lo que van a hacer. Es lo que van a hacer.
Para que mi honey me venga a ver."
~Wally Gonzales, The Short-Legged Texan

A "new" pair of sneakers
The latest full features
The parking's free, ya vente!

A '94 Nissan
Pero sin transmichian
Your Tío Frank can fix it

St. Patrick's Day lights
Some Clinton/Gore kites
A wrist-watch/television

En la pulga se halla, se compra, se vende
Lo que pide la gente!

Aquí tienen Legos
Carritos y juegos
I want a spiropapa

Aguacates, nopales
Te llenan morrales
Con fruits y vegetales

Llantas pa' tus trailes
Los domingos hay bailes
Te ponen windshield wipers

En la pulga se halla, se compra, se vende
Lo que pide la gente!

Yo quiero gorditas
Arroz y carnitas
Frijoles a la charra

Taquitos al gusto
Te curan del susto
La lady da sobadas

Un hotdog con todo
Si me muero, ni modo
También venden coronas

En la pulga se halla, se compra, se vende
Lo que pide la gente!

En la pulga se halla, se compra, se vende
Lo que pide la gente!

QUESTIONS

1. What is the official language of the United States of America?
2. How does the author use humor to relate the theme of the poem?
3. How would you describe the author's use of rhyme?
4. The "coronas" in the poem are funeral wreaths—not beers. How do mistranslations lead to complications?
5. What is the value of bilingualism or multilingualism?
6. The author's book description states that he uses code-switching in part to entertain and in part to challenge his boundaries as a writer, to stretch his vocal chords, so to speak, but also in part to challenge the lingering prejudice against such mestizaje--or meeting and mixing of cultures (and also voices)--and help convert our society into one that accepts itself as it is: polyglossic and stronger for it." How does this poem help accomplish the author's stated purpose?
7. What is empowering about this poem?

Clean-up: Table Five

One night at eight as we ate chicken soup
She had me pay for dinner, like a dupe—
This, after breaking up with me in front
Of strangers at a crowded restaurant.
To add insult to injury she asked
For me to drive her home that night and laughed
In glory at her triumph over love.
My heart, it stood, a loaded dove
Now caged, now maimed, now shot out recklessly
Against the door of opportunity.
I shall be telling this along with sighs—
I miss the road diverged between her thighs.
Though ne'er did love a heart as true as mine.
She was replaced a quarter after nine.

QUESTIONS

1. What figures of speech do you experience in the poem?
2. What allusions do you recognize in the poem?
3. How would you describe the tone of the poem?
4. Does this poem qualify as a sonnet?
5. How does the title fit the poem?
6. What is empowering about this poem?

In-A-God, A-New-Vita

Poor wretch. It refused team in shores.
Why people want to come here, I don't know.
Crashing mosaic fluttering destiny,
Ramp and in dull gent strangers energized by time

Why people want to come here? I don't! No!
Instinctive double-cross of oceans leaves. Love's behind.
Rampant indulgent strangers, energized, buy time.
Into one another we must feed.

Instinctive doubt. Crossing ocean leaves loves behind.
Hunt and gather luggage, gun, and blanket.
In two, one.   Another we must feed.
Compass, compact Bible, community.

Hunt and gather lug. Gauge gun and blank it.
Faceless names on tiered family trees.
Come. Pass. Come, packed Bible. Come, Unity.
Genetic disconnection—planned in retrospect.

Face less names.   On, tired family trees!
Foreign heirs air different goals.
Genetic disc connection planned in retro specs.
Poor: wretched refuse teaming shores.

QUESTIONS

1. What characteristics of a pantoum do you recognize in the poem?
2. What allusions do you recognize in the poem?
3. How would you describe the theme of the poem?
4. What is empowering about this poem?

Cafecito
(parody of "Despacito")

Sí,
sabes que ya llevo un friegos esperandote
Tengo que wake up contigo hoy

Vi,
the pot is empty y estaba enojandome
If you drink the last cup rinse it, yo!

Tú, tú eres el jarabe que quiero probar
Me voy acercando para el counter man
This line is too long y eso no es justo (Oh no)

I, I can't wait to hold you in my burning hand
Now my little heart is beating really fast.
Esto hay que tomármelo oscuro y puro

CA-FE-CITO
Quiero respirar tu aroma sabrocito
Men like Juan Valdez te piscan despacito
Con canela, crema, o bien sencillito

CA-FE-CITO
La dulce amargura de un Cubanito
Negro, azucarado, y bien calientito
Mexican, Columbian, Americanito

(Gimme, gimme, gimme! Gimme, gimme, gimme!)

I wanna see you roasted up
I wanna hear you grindin'
I want you to wake up my taste buds
So they're no longer deaf and blinded

I wanna spill your beans
I wanna feel you steamin'
I want your coffee pot to wake me
From the nightmare I been dreamin'

I know Starbucks be milkin' it
I know e'rybody thinkin' it
Starbucks makin' a killin'
'Cause chumps like us be willin'

I know I can save some money, baby—dumb, dumb
I know my bank account be wiggin', baby—dumb, dumb

I came up to the Dark Side knowing that it's evil
You don't have to judge me 'cause this stuff is legal
I got issues, Baby, I know got baggage!
I try to drink it slow, but then I get all savage!

Espre-, espressito coffee tan dulcito
I'm getting addicted slowly, al poquito
When you kiss my lips like sweet cappuccino
You're making me an offer like I'm Al Pacino

Espre-, espressito coffee tan dulcito
We're getting together, like un puzzle-sito
Gives me an excuse to have some pastelito
It's the only way to eat some pan dulcito!

CA-FE-CITO
Quiero respirar tu aroma sabrocito
Men like Juan Valdez te piscan despacito
Con canela, crema, o bien sencillito

CA-FE-CITO
La dulce amargura de un Folgerito
Negro, azucarado, y bien calientito

French, Arabian, Swiss, or Indonesiancito

(Gimme, gimme, gimme! Gimme, gimme, gimme!)

I wanna see you roasting up
I wanna hear you grindin'
I want you to wake up my taste buds
So they're no longer deaf and blinded

I wanna spill your beans
I wanna feel you steamin'
I want your coffee pot to wake me
From the nightmare I've been dreamin'

CA-FE-CITO
Please don't talk to me until my first traguito
I like it cowboy style with some tocinito
Can I get an Amen?! Can I get a grito?!

Espre-espressito coffee tan dulcito
I'm getting addicted slowly, al poquito

I wanna see you roasting up
I wanna hear you grindin'

Espre-, espressito coffee tan dulcito
We're getting together, like un puzzle-sito

I want you to wake up my taste buds
So they're no longer deaf and blinded

QUESTIONS

1. What characteristics of a parody do you recognize in the poem?
2. What allusions do you recognize in the poem?
3. What role does code-switching play in the poem?
4. What is empowering about this poem?

Songs of Fight or Flight

"You may encounter many defeats, but you must
not be defeated. In fact, it may be necessary to
encounter the defeats so you can know who
you are, what you can rise from,
how you can still come
out of it."
~ Maya Angelou

Immigrant Crossing

My father's feet
Carried the sesquicentennial stench of
Mexico, turned Texas, turned United States of America.

He labored in 24- and 48-hour shifts
Irrigating arid citrus groves,
Working under the bellies of navel orchards
In trenches that emanated a stink
That America could not stomach.

Mother Nature painted on my father's immigrant feet
Socks of earth, wind, and tire,
Then drowned them in her melting pot,

Ankles aching,
Bunions burning,
Blisters bleeding,
Calluses calcificating,
Nails embedded with myriad funguses
Frolicking frivolously
Only to become penitent parasites.

My father left
Mexticacán, Jalisco—
Less than a spec
On the Mexican map—
And crossed the Rio Grande
For the privilege of standing on American soil,
For the privilege of owning an American acre,
For the privilege of raising his American children,
For the privilege of ruling
Over endless, waveless American ditches

On toasty Texas summer nights
When he'd come home at dawn,
We knew he was home upon smell,
As he shed his black boots
With a sigh of repose,
Crossing his feet
Under Uncle Sam's nose.

QUESTIONS

1. The author takes liberties in spelling to create a desired sound or rhythm or effect. What is the effect of stretching the boundaries of language in creative works?
2. What figures of speech do you experience in the poem?
3. What allusions do you recognize in the poem?
4. What is the overarching tone detected in the poem?
5. How does this poem relate to the section title: Songs of Fight or Flight?
6. What is empowering about this poem?

La Labor: Migrantes del Valle

I woke daily to the sound of my mother's wooden *palote*
gliding over the kitchen counter, where she flattened
the hand-kneaded dough to make flour tortillas.

Beans and tortillas. Tortillas con beans. Beans con frijoles.
Tacos wrapped in foil paper to keep them warm,
Wrapped in foil to keep away dust, bugs, hunger.

We dressed in long-sleeved shirts and hats, and raced
the sun through curving forest roads and drove.

Sometimes, Tío Rico would stop to fire at a deer
no one else saw from his window. And we drove.

We picked tiny cucumbers for pickling—
their thorny fuzz befriending our skin—
in a clumsy squatted waltz in the fog through endless rows
of green and dirt and sun.

We picked asparagus.
Cleaned rows between potato plants, radishes.
We picked banana peppers. Packed potatoes. And drove.
Our fingers smelled of dirt and pesticides.
There was no bathroom in the fields.

The day never ended.

All summer was one day and every day was workday.
'Apá would dip our sodas in a cold creek.
We worked and couldn't wait for lunch time—
at 10 a.m.

Once, with nothing else to eat in sight,
Nena and I devoured saltine crackers dipped in chocolate

frosting.
I was eight.

We'd get back to camp and eat and shower and sleep and begin again.

Sometimes George would catch frogs at the canal before dinner.
Sometimes Arturo would run with Licha from Edinburg, who was in Cross Country and had nice legs.

The few Sundays when we didn't work all day we played baseball.
Mom hit a homerun.
Dad played cards until two in the morning.
Marco was his good-luck charm.
Tío Rico danced with a goat on dad's birthday—
and then cooked it.

Minnesota. Wisconsin. Arkansas. Texas.

I hated interstate truck stops
with lights like a surgeon's lamp
that startled us awake.
I feared the spaghetti crisscross highways,
the tall overpasses of the big cities.

One year, on our way home, our station wagon burned.
The engine overheated. The grass caught fire.
Mom saved a blanket she was knitting.
The ball of yarn rolled out of the car, aflame.
My mother prayed about it.
My father wrote a song.
Tío Rico cursed.
The kids cried.
Max's fishing rods melted to the car.

Half of what we'd earned burned
with that avocado green station wagon
We moved on.

We were split up and got a ride to the next migrant camp
from strangers.
A black trucker dropped off three of us in Hope.
I don't remember how we got home to Texas.

Back home, every season had its crop
Every Saturday its early start.
We picked onions and onions and onions and
cantaloupes and tomatoes and oranges and grapefruits
and onions.

When the teacher asked me to write about where we had
gone
during our summer "vacation"
I always said the same thing:

Nowhere.

QUESTIONS

1. What figures of speech do you experience in the poem?
2. How does this poem connect with the Mexican American immigrant experience?
5. What is the overarching tone detected in the poem?
6. How does this poem relate to the section title: Songs of Fight or
7. Flight?
8. What is empowering about this poem?

El Muro: The New Colossus
(After Emma Lazarus)

Though data demands that I exist
My mathematics do not compute
Programmed to divide
Instead I subtract

I keep the cats of prey encaged
I keep the flightless birds enslaved
I give no life
I am ashamed

No songs I raise
No water flows
I block the ways
I seal the door

I find solace in the sighs of the wind
Caressing my iron beaded seams
I find mercy in the beating sun
Tanning my hide, my dying dreams

I cry no peals of joy at church
Nor *slip the surly bonds of earth*
I sail no fair-wind open sea
I live to kill
In infamy

Not a bridge
Not a tower
Not a soul
Just a briar

I hide my lamp
Beside the golden door

Since those like you
Aren't welcome anymore

QUESTIONS

1. What figures of speech do you experience in the poem?
2. How does the poem assist the reader in recognizing the allusions in the poem?
3. Who (or what) acts as the speaker of the poem?
4. Who is the audience being directly addressed in the poem?
5. What is the overarching tone detected in the poem?
6. What is the significance of the poet deciding to use almost no punctuation marks?
7. What is empowering about this poem?

*In America**

technology has evolved
racist people have not

superimposed images on maps
they created of lands they did not

real people have also appeared
on this continent

a regular paradise
in the Land of the Gorch

with no puppeteer in sight
no papers

only their underwear and hopes—
the Electric Mayhem continues

*(a found poem from an article about Jim Henson's Muppets and Sesame Street. Italicized words are from the article.)

QUESTIONS

1. What is the effect of the poet's minimalist approach with this poem?
2. How does the poem reveal the American immigrant experience?
3. What is the overarching tone detected in the poem?
4. What is empowering about this poem?

Coatlicue: Blues *Do* Be A Mockingbird

"Music was my refuge. I could crawl into
the space between the notes and curl
my back to loneliness."
~ Maya Angelou

Just Selfies
(For Vincent)

What wondrous strokes we might behold.
What enchanted lights and curves and swirls
upon a woman's naked bosom or smooth, bent back.
The artist's loving hand turned flowers into gold,
self-portraits filled with agony untold,
abandoned streets of old into romantic
boulevards of broken screams.
But Van Gogh's night scenes starred no starlets.
Painted ladies don't jut out from his canvases.
Gaugin offered no large nudes on loan.
What they don't tell you about Vincent
is that his brushes stroked no hips.
What they don't dare mention
is the violence and the fits.
What they don't like to talk about
is the depression and the ticks.
Crazy doesn't sell until the paint is dry
and the body has been tagged.

QUESTIONS

1. Why is it important for a society to support its artists?
2. How would you describe the author's use of rhyme?
3. What poetic elements do you experience in the poem?
4. This section, Coatlicue: Blues Do Be A Mockingbird, alludes to Anzaldúa's writings on the state of depression. How does this poem connect to that state of being?
5. What is empowering about this poem?

WRITING PROMPT

Attempt an ekphrastic writing by viewing an unknown work of visual art: a sculpture, a photograph, a painting, or film, then write a journal entry, a quick-write, a made-up story, or a poem.

But You Don't Date Guys Like That

He wants to love you

like a death row inmate loves
    the sun, the pain of knowing

like suicide bombers love
    martyrdom, the smell of burning flesh

like a butterfly loves
    nectar, the caress of the wind

like America loves
    Chipotle, cultural appropriation

like Juárez loves
    tequila, butchering women

like Austin loves
    food trucks, gentrification

like Chicago loves
    deep-dish pizza, murder

like Los Angeles loves
    itself.

He would miss you like

a metaphor misses like, or as

a racist misses George Wallace, or as

the sand dunes miss the waves, or as

a new mother misses the weight, or as

a bullet misses the dark, still
smell inside a fully-loaded gun
under a motel pillow.

QUESTIONS

1. What is the effect of the poet's minimalist approach with this poem?
2. What poetic elements do you experience in this poem?
3. What allusions do you recognize in the poem?
4. How does the title of the poem connect to its theme?
5. How does the poem reveal the speaker's a sense of humor?
6. What is empowering about this poem?

My Dearest Nadine
(Inspired by the film "Drugstore Cowboy")

I want to carry you
In my arms and steal you away
Throw you over my shoulder
Drop you as gentle
As a pillowcase full of yesterday's downy dreams
Bury you in a light blue bag
In a perfectly rectangular pit
Dug deep within a green wood of pines and ferns
That smells of gleaming checkered floors in rundown
    theaters
Mopped into forgetting the bloody stains of slit throats and
burst veins and ashes.

I want to take you for a scenic drive
Down a muddy back-road in Oregon
Lay you down where unseen birds will serenade you sweet
    lullabies
Pat the earth smooth and cross myself and just walk away—
Away from spinning hats and blue skies and all—
Hop back on my old green truck
Shove off without a word
Like a drugstore cowboy
Forget about the whole thing
Drive off into the sun
Set my eyes on the fast-fading horizon
In the rearview mirror
And be good. Be a regular guy.

QUESTIONS
1. What is ironic about this poem?
2. What poetic elements do you experience in this poem?
3. Describe the poet's use of juxtaposition in the poem.
4. Why is it healthy to write about dark issues?
5. What is empowering about this poem?

Songs of Mourning

"History, despite its wrenching pain, cannot be unlived, but, if faced with courage, need not be lived again."

"No matter what happens,
or how bad it seems today,
life does go on,
and it will be better tomorrow."
~ Maya Angelou

A Time For Mourning

Time heals no wounds.

Pain never dies.

Time flies, and with it, pain little by little subsides, but there’s no expiration date on pain and there's no term limit on mourning. Period.

It's not easy letting go, and it's absolutely not required.

Even when your heart is broken, the sun will rise, beautiful and pink and orange and purple and warm but the grief is not retired.

Morning leads to morning as mourning leads to mourning and the pain you thought was naught will come back without warning.

You'll cry for the moment. You’ll cry for the memories.

Sadness will hit you in unexpected places on unexpected days: on days when the sun is shining and when clouds fill the sky, in the third inning of a baseball game and at halftime during football season, when your son holds your hand in a parking lot, or when your daughter goes off to college.

Time heals no wounds.

Pain never dies.

Time flies, and with it, pain little by little subsides.

QUESTIONS

1. Is it okay to be sad?
2. What poetic elements do you experience in this poem?
3. What is the tone of the poem?
4. What is empowering about this poem?

London: July 7, 2005

The Union Jack flew proudly in the breeze at 8:51 in the morning.

They were on their way to work at 8:51 in the morning.

The first bombs exploded at 8:51 in the morning.

The underground tunnels shook at 8:51 in the morning.

They didn't know what hit 'em at 8:51 in the morning.

It was hard to breathe in the trains at 8:51 in the morning.

The passengers cried out loud at 8:51 in the morning.

The faces and the streets were bloody at 8:51 in the morning.

They took pictures with their cell phones at 8:51 in the morning.

The bobbies ran and the ambulances rolled at 8:51 in the morning.

Nurses ran to help the wounded at 8:51 in the morning.

They performed C.P.R. on the street at 8:51 in the morning.

They pulled the dead from the trains at 8:51 in the morning.

They prayed to God at 8:51 in the morning.

The Pope blessed himself   at 8:51 in the morning.

They searched the debris for clues   at 8:51 in the morning.

The terrorists pissed me off   at 8:51 in the morning.

They shouted, "Bloody Bastards!"   at 8:51 in the morning.

The world got a little smaller   at 8:51 in the morning.

Strangers held each other close   at 8:51 in the morning.

The English roses wilted   at 8:51 in the morning.

The sun still kept rising   at 8:51 in the morning.

QUESTIONS

1. Is anger a healthy response to tragedy?
2. What is the effect of the author's use of caesura?
3. What poetic elements do you experience in this poem?
4. What is the tone of the poem?
5. What is empowering about this poem?

Deadlines: The Tragedy of Media-crity
(Sandy Hook: December 14, 2012)

They will rank you
They will Connecticut you down to palatable pieces of
footage
A-B-C-and-D-roll through your town
They will calculate and hope to see you
Make the top-five school massacres of all time—
Other countries need not apply—
They will synonymize you in perpetuity with Columbine,
Virginia Tech,
And some other third shooting they'll have to google

They will rank you
On a slow news day, they will thank you
For becoming the lead
Story after story after story
They will file you
They will roll up and down the town
And profile you
Run an exposé on every mother-father-sister-brother and
defile you
Interview your neighbor, your friend, your enemy, your dog
Salivate at the chance to out your every indiscretion
Make you the cause of the killer's transgression
Veil thin your every sin

They will rank you
They will list and classify and bank you—
The victims and the families
The survivors and fatalities
The heroes and the wannabes

They will rank you
They will heatedly discuss you

Over pictures, fonts, and headlines
They will credit and discredit you
Plaster your picture in the paper
Check Wikipedia for a connection to the date
Check Facebook profiles for tell-tale signs of hate

They will rank you
They will dramatize and victimize and sterilize you
Until the death-weary world retracts
Until the next celebrity drunk attacks
Until the next death do you part
Until the next anniversary
Then the five-and-ten-year mark

QUESTIONS

1. Discuss the poet's play on words in the poem.
2. Whom is the speaker addressing?
3. How does the speaker describe the media's response to mass shootings?
4. How would you describe the author's use of rhyme?
5. What figures of speech do you experience in the poem?
6. What allusions do you recognize in the poem?
7. What is the speaker's overall tone?
8. What is empowering about this poem?

Autumn: Massacre In Paris
(Le 13 Novembre, 2015)

I.
Leaves change: fall.

II.
Leaves change fall.

III.
Fall change leaves.

IV.
Change leaves.
Fall.

V.
Fall leaves change.

VI.
Fall leaves.
Change.

VII.
Change.
Fall.
(Leaves.)

QUESTIONS

1. Discuss the poet's play on words in the poem.
2. Whom is the speaker addressing?
3. Describe the poet's use of syntax to reveal meaning.
4. Describe the poet's use of polysemic language.
5. What is empowering about this poem?

Songs of Praise

"Let gratitude be the pillow upon which you kneel to say your nightly prayer. And let faith be the bridge you build to overcome evil and welcome good."
~Maya Angelou

Left-Centered, Right Justified

Leftists are communist pinkos.
Guerrilleros

Zurdos
Malcriados
Looking for a handout
Siniestro/Sinister/
Liberal global warming *propagandistas*
Leftistas barristas

Centrists are lukewarm.
Neither hot nor cold
Just fine for Goldilocks,
Not good enough for Martin
Como los hermaphrodites
Ni de aqui, ni de alla
Playing for both teams
Passive-Aggressive Reformist-Conservatives
Republicrats/Demopublicans
Philaphobes/Phobiaphiles
Ché/Hitler Hybrids
"I voted for it
before I voted against it."
Peaceful Warriors
Seriously Funny
Simple Genius

Rightist are mightists
Under a conservative light
Kristallnacht/Crystal Night
Right to life/Right to bear arms
God and country

Dextro/*Derecho*/Right
Nazis *supremecistas*
Fascistas capitalistas

A n d e v e r y o n e f e e l s t o t a l m e n t e j u s t i f i e d .

Good thing God is *bien trucha con* Word!

QUESTIONS

1. Discuss the poet's play on words in the poem.
2. What allusions do you recognize in the poem?
3. What role does code-switching play in the poem?
4. Describe the poet's use of syntax to reveal meaning.
5. What is empowering about this poem?

Creation

in seven days God
made the universe divine
nature in its prime

QUESTIONS

1. Discuss the poet's play on words in the poem.
2. What allusions do you recognize in the poem?
3. How does the poem's title connect with the section title?
4. What is empowering about this poem?

WRITING PROMPT

What do you believe in? Journal. Write a list. Convert your ideas into a poem about your beliefs.

Numbered Days

I see

The crashing hours
Upon the sands of time,

The crested days and
Weeks and waves
Ending with a sigh,

The roaring months
And rolling years
Waving their goodbye,
Tossed in
metronomic pace—

Empty as they lie.
And on that calm horizon
Where God threw down His rock,
Where tidal ripples started,
The end of time is nigh.

QUESTIONS

1. What is the connection between the poem's title and its theme?
2. How would you describe the poet's use of rhyme?
3. Discuss the poet's play on words in the selection.
4. What is the effect of line spacing or shape?
5. What is empowering about this poem?

Time Is Manna

Time is a sustenance that cannot be hoarded.
The end of time will never be recorded.
Time soothes the aches that
come from great mistakes.
To spend time is a virtue.
To waste time is human.
To give time is divine.
Time can't be bought.
Time can't be sold.
Time is ever on
the horizon.
Time
is
Love.
Time has
No heir, no care,
Absolutely no despair.
Time is a harsh extorter.
Time is a gentle exhorter.
Time cannot be recreated.
Time cannot be destroyed.
Time is always never late.
Time is karma's incubator.
Time is the rarest jewel to behold.
Time is Manna, a providence of Heaven.

QUESTIONS

1. What is the connection between the poem's shape and its theme?
2. How would you describe the poet's use of rhyme?
3. What is empowering about this poem?

Bendición en el Sillón
*(Blessing on the Sofa)

Que fregado de mí
Hoy yo amanecí
Sin tortillas, sin pan, sin café.

How miserable of me
For today I awoke
Sans tortillas, sans bread,
sans coffee.

A la calle salí
Casi de hambre morí
Y a la casa de empeño yo fui.

I took to the street
Almost starving to death
And straight to the pawn
shop I went.

Puse en empeño
A un jalapeño

There, I pawned
A lone jalapeño pepper

Y un nicle me dio el señor.

And a nickel the man
gave to me.

Con el nicle compre
un taco al pastor
Que sin chile no tenía sabor

With the nickel I bought
a barbecue taco
That, sans chile, much
flavor lacked.

A la casa volví
Y con gran frenesí
De rodillas le ore al Señor,

To my house I returned
And with a great frenzy
On my knees I prayed to
the Lord,

Y el Señor contesto,
"¿No te he dicho que Yo
Sere tu Proveedor?"

And the Lord answered,
"Have I not said that I
Shall be your Great
Provider?"

En el viejo sillón
Me halle un tostón
Y de pronto a la tienda corrí.

In the aged sofa
I found a half-dollar
And then hurriedly ran

	to the store.
Que dichoso de mí	How lucky of me
Ya que tengo aquí	Now that I have with me
Mis tortillas, mi pan, y mi fe.	My tortillas, my bread, and my faith.

*(Poem loosely translated from the original Spanish version to English by the author.)

QUESTIONS

1. What role does the speaker's faith play in characterization?
2. How does the author use humor to relate the theme of the poem?
3. How would you describe the author's use of rhyme?
4. What is empowering about this poem?

Heaven Sent

Days of old
Prophets speak.
Babe foretold.
People seek.

Shepherds slept. Angels sang. Promise kept.
Behold the Lamb!
Virgin-born. Wise Men seek. Star-adorned.
Born so meek.
Dove soared. Heaven sent. Called the Lord.
Knees are bent.
Truth restored. Folks repent. Crowd adored.
Lame men leapt.

Demons warred.
Cup accept.
Crowd roared.
Mother wept.
Maimed and gored.
Christ crept.
Mocked and scorned.
Silence kept.
Nailed to board.

Skin torn.
Christ forgives.
Crown of thorns.
Thief lives.

God disowned.
Angels mourned.
Sin atoned.
Christ entombed.

Darkness ends.
Third day rose.
Christ ascends.
Living prose.

QUESTIONS

1. What is the significance of the number of lines in the poem?
2. How is the poet's use of shape and syntax connected to the theme of the poem?
3. How would you describe the author's use of rhyme?
4. What is empowering about this poem?

WRITING PROMPTS

1. What would you be willing to sacrifice for those you love?
2. Write a poem based on the shape of the topic of your poem.

The Beginning and The End

In the End
I will want nothing,
for I shall have it all

In the End
Everything I now own
I shall never need again

In the End
I will love perfectly
and be
wise,
beautiful,
holy,
complete

In the End
I shall be your child
and you shall be my God,
and therefore,

My Beginning

QUESTIONS

1. How would you describe the speaker of the poem?
2. Discuss the author's use of paradox.
3. What is empowering about this poem?

WRITING PROMPTS

1. Is death the end of all?
2. What does your faith teach about the afterlife?

Encore: Dial "M" For Mexican

"Love is a condition so powerful; it may be that which pulls the stars in the firmament. It may be that which pushes and urges the blood in the veins. Courage: you have to have courage to love somebody because you risk everything—everything."
~ Maya Angelou

ROMEO & JULIET *¿Y QUÉ?*

A Reimagined and Adapted Scene

In Chicano Caló, Tex-Mex,

Spanish, and English

ROMEO & JULIET ¿Y QUÉ?

A one-scene adaptation of Act I, Scene 5 of William Shakespeare's "Romeo & Juliet" reimagined as a contemporary *fiesta* attended by two competing cholo gang/families in an American Latino/Hispanic/Mexican American community.

Characters:

CAPULET: *El mero-mero chingón*; father of JULIET; 60

EL VIEJO CAPULET: Old-School *Cholo* in a zoot-suit; wears an Army Vietnam medal; 65+

LA JULIET: beautiful, young jail bait; *hija* de CAPULET; 13

TYBALT: lieutenant of CAPULET; *sobrino* by marriage; 18

ROMEO *MONTESCO*: handsome son of CAPULET's rival; 16

BENVOLIO: *primo* and best friend of ROMEO; 17

LA NURSE: Older lady; only woman wearing a dress or nightgown—with shawl; indigenous/bronze skin; 55

GUESTS--*VATOS LOCOS & CHICAS SUAVES*

VATOS LOCOS: Men of different ages—though mostly younger, mostly muscular, wearing well-dressed and pressed *cholo* attire; some wear zoot-suits (partial or full); some have their top button buttoned—but none other, and the shirt's untucked. Some have visible tattoos; aged 14 to 45

CHICAS SUAVES: Women of different ages, shapes, and sizes, dressed as cholas (no dresses) in t-shirts or muscle shirts, some with jeans and some with khakis, with *chola* eyebrows and make-up, including blue or pink eye-shadow. Some have tattoos; aged 15 to 45

LOS SERVINGMEN: Young muscular men wearing white muscle shirts, matching khaki pants, black suspenders, hair nets, and Stacey Adams shoes; aged 14—33

Setting:

Party at CAPULET's house. Evening.

Time:

The present.

Act I, Scene Five:

At Rise: CAPULET stands facing stage left, greeting the GUESTS (who spread out and mingle inaudibly throughout the stage after being greeted by CAPULET, who poses occasionally with GUESTS for a camera (flashing OFFSTAGE). CAPULET greets the *VATOS LOCOS* with a combination of handshakes and half-hugs and with bows and kissing of hands or kisses on the cheek for the *CHICAS SUAVES*. *LOS* SERVINGMEN pace hither-thither, some carrying serving trays and occasionally handing bottled beer to other GUESTS, JULIET, *LA* NURSE, and TYBALT, who are already inside the *fiesta*. Party music can be heard in the background. A *VATO LOCO* who's shirtless in the corner is cornering a *CHICA SUAVE*.

(Entran CAPULET, *EL VIEJO* CAPULET, *LA* JULIET, TYBALT, *LA* NURSE, *LOS* SERVINGMEN, and *todos los* GUESTS--*VATOS LOCOS & CHICAS SUAVES al pori*.)

CAPULET

¿Qué onda, Carnal?

(Poses for the camera with *VATO LOCO* and other GUESTS; returns attention to others.)

Ey, Homes!

(Greets a *VATO LOCO*; resumes attention to others.)

¡Bienvenidos a todos! ¡Aquí están en su cantón, Ese!

(Poses for the camera with *VATO LOCO* and other GUESTS; returns to others.)

Las chachitas que no tienen callos en sus dedos bailarán con ustedes. 'Hora sí, mis jainas, ¿quién de ustedes se negará a zapatear? Ajúa! El que no se ponga a tirar chancla, le diré a todo mundo que tienen callos. ¿No que no, cabrones? ¡Órale! ¡Pónganse! ¡A bailar se ha dicho! 'Sup, *carnal? Nombre yo antes también me ponía a menear el bote, pero* it's been a while, Homes. *Yo hace un friegos que supe cómo hacerle pedo a las chavalónas.* I could whisper some sweet something-something in a honey's *oidito,* you know. *Pero, chale, Ese. Ese tiempo ya paso pa' mí.* I'm too old for that! Ey, come in, *Carnal*! ¡*Todos son* welcome! Ey, deejay, *ponle, Carnal*! ¡*Haste garras!*

(Music plays, and they dance. To the SERVINGMEN)

¡Hagan campo! ¡Muevan ese pedo!

(To the *CHICAS SUAVES*)

¡Órale, rukas, shake those *nalgitas!*

(To *LOS* SERVINGMEN)

¡E, güey! ¡Más luz acá, baboso! ¡Limpien las mesas y muévanlas pa' allá! ¡Y apaga esa lumbre! ¿No vez que 'ta muy hot? *¡Este vato!*

(To his CAPULET CUZ)

¿Qué onda? ¡Primo! 'Ta con madre este pori, que no? ¡Nombre siéntate, güey! ¡Hijuesú! ¡Ya 'tamos too old *pa' este pedo!*

(CAPULET and his COUSIN sit down)

¿Desde cuándo que no nos vemos en un borlo como este?

EL VIEJO CAPULET

Te lo juro que ya hace un treintón de años, Homes.

CAPULET

¡Chale, Cuz! *Nombre, ¡no mames! ¡No es pa' tanto! Wátchale: ¡la última vez fue en el* wedding *de Lucho! Yo sé que el tiempo pasa en friegas, pero son hace* 25 years ago, *¿qué no?*

EL VIEJO CAPULET

¡Nel pastel! Son más, ¡Primo! ¡Son más! ¡Al hijo de Lucho ya le cuelgan, Carnal! ¡Ya cumplió treinta años el dude!

CAPULET

¡A la mo! *¿En serio,* Homes? *¡Su hijo era un chavalón hace dos años!*

ROMEO

(To A SERVINGMAN)

Ey, *Vato, ¿quién es esa* chick *hablando con aquel dude?*

SERVINGMAN

Sepa la mo, *Carnal.*

ROMEO

Ssss. ¡Mamacita! ¡Da más luz que un cuete en el 4th of July! *No es de Dios. 'Ta demasiado buenona pa' esta vida!* Damn! That baby doll is too damn fine *pa' que la entierren cuando muera! 'Ta hecha pa' dar luz a las estrellas! ¡Se ve más puri que un* dove *entre cuervos! Cuando se acabe esta* song, *la wa seguir a ver que ondón. Hijuesú!* I never been *enamorado* like this! *Mis* eyes *me mintieron antes.* I never been in love *hasta 'horita!*

TYBALT

Que jodidos? Ey! I know that voice! *Este vato es un Montesco.*

(To his PAGE)

¡Tráeme mi daga, Ese!

(*Bien* angry.)

¿Qué jodidos hace aquí ese méndigo con su cara escondida en una mask? *¿Cómo se atreve el güey? ¡Me lo voy a destrampar pa' que se le quite!*

CAPULET

Ey, *quihúbole, Sobrinito?* Why you mad, Bro?

TYBALT

¡Tío, este vato es un Montesco – nuestro enemigo! ¡Es un canalla que vino a fregar con nosotros aquí en tu chánte!

CAPULET

¿Ese dude *es el tal Romeo?*

TYBALT

¡Simón que sí, Tío! That's the *sanavabiche!*

CAPULET

¡Calmantes montes, Carnal-ation! *Tíralo al león y no te agüites. Dicen que este vato no es mala onda.* I hear *que* he's actually a pretty chill dude, T-Dog, so *no te esponjes,* Cuz. *No quiero pedo aquí en mi borlo,* so *ponte al alba y respétame,* Homes. *Ponte las pilas y aliviánate, ¡¿okay?!*

TYBALT

¡¿Cómo que no me voy a esponjar con ese canalla aquí, Tío?! He shouldn't be here, ey! It's our party!

CAPULET

I already said *que* he can stay, Homes, so chill out, *Ese*! *¡Ya hablé! ¡¿Qué jodidos? ¡¿Aquí yo mando, que no?! ¡No seas soflamero! ¡Si empiezas pedo con todo mundo* it's gonna be your fault, not mine! *¡No quiero bronca en mi cantón, Ese!*

TYBALT

Yeah, but, . . . *¡Tío, . . . pos* . . . he's disrespecting us!

CAPULET

¿Quién chinga'os te crées, huerco mocoso? Are you being for real, *Vato*? *¿Te creés el mero mero fregón o qué? ¡Mira, Sobrinito, ya te he dicho que conmigo se te nubla, cabrón! No me vuelvas a rezongár* or I will kick your ass right here in front of your homies, ey!

(To *los* GUESTS)

¡Simón! Ta bien de aquellas, Carnal! That's bad ass, ey!

(To TYBALT)

¡¿Entonces que, güey? ¡Ponte trucha o te descuento! You hearing me, Foo?

(To los SERVINGMEN)

Hey, *Ese*, more light over here, Foo! *'Ta bien* dark *aquí*!

(To TYBALT)

'Che huerco mocoso sin vergüenza! ¡Te me callas el hocico y te me largas a la fregada, or else, *Ese*! You feel me, Homes?

(to the GUESTS)

Órale, Ese! Échenle ganas, Carnal! ¡A bailar se ha dicho! Ajúa!

(*La música* continúes *y los* GUESTS *bailan.*)

TYBALT

¡Me tiembla el pinche cuerpo como perro enrabiado! ¡Me wa ir, ey, . . . *pero este pedo que por 'horita le parece bien* sweet *a* Romeo *le va* taste-*iar amargo al güey!* Laterz, Homes!

(*Se va el* TYBALT *bien* pissed off, all *sentido el* dude.)

ROMEO

(Takes JULIET's hand.)

Tu mano es como un holy place *que mi mano no debe tocar. Pero si te ofendes que te 'toy tochando con mi* hand, *pos mis* two lips *aquí están listitos como los* pilgrims *pa'* fix-*iarlo con un besito,*

¡ey!

JULIET

Cálmate, Homes. *¡No manches! Dale un poco de* credit *a tus manos.* By holding my hand *me enseñas respeto, y, pos, al fin, los* pilgrims *tochan las manos de las* statues *de los santitos, ¿qué no? Poniendo una* palm *contra otra* palm *es como un besito,* ¿ey?

ROMEO

¿Qué no tienen los santitos y los pilgrims lips *también?*

JULIET

¡Simón, Ese! – pero esos lips *los usan los* pilgrims *pa' orar.*

ROMEO

Pues entonces 'ira, Santita: deja que tus lips *hagan lo que hacen tus* hands. *'Toy orando que me des un besito. Dame mi oración pa' que no cambie mi fe por desesperación.*

JULIET

Los santos no se hacen move, *ni hasta cuando conceden una oración.*

ROMEO

Pos entonces no te hagas move *mientras tomo el efecto de mi oracioncita.*

(*Le da un* kiss *a la* chick.)

¡'Hora sí! You took my sin *de mis* lips *con tus* lips.

JULIET

¡Híjole! ¿Y a poco tienen mis lips *el* sin *que te quitaron?*

ROMEO

¿El sin *de mis* lips? That's *firme*! *Me animas que sea un* smooth criminal *con tu dulzura. ¡Regrésame mi* sin *pa' 'tras!*

(*Otro* Kiss.)

JULIET

Hijuesú! ¡Besas con madre!

NURSE

Ey, *¡Mi 'ja, te habla tu 'Amá!*

(JULIET *se va* to the side.)

ROMEO

¿Quién es su 'Amá?

NURSE

A lo mero macho, Hijo, su jefita es la mera señora del cantón. Es bien de aquellas. Yo mismito le di pecho a su hija cuando estaba chiquitirrina. Wátchate, deja te digo algo, ey: *¡el vato* that marries *esta rukita le va caér un diablaso de lana! Te digo que se va a rifar. ¡La mera neta,* ey!

ROMEO

(To himself)

Más triste! Hijuesú! 'Toy bien salado! ¿Es Capuleta? ¡Me lleva San Gaspar! ¡Mi vida loca is now in the hands *de mi enemiga chaparrita!*

BENVOLIO

(To ROMEO)

¡Ponte trucha, Carnal! Vámonos antes de que se ponga malo este pedo!

ROMEO

Simón, Ese. Ya se pone tristón este pedo.

CAPULET

¿Qué onda, muchachos? ¿Cómo que ya se van? ¡To'avía falta la tragazón!

(They whisper in his ear *que* it's late, so *ya estufas – ya es muy tarde el pedo.)*

¡A la mo! *Bueno pues,* thank you for coming, ¿ey? *¡En serio, Carnalitos! ahí nos watchamos,* Homes. *Buenas noches a todo mundo. ¡Ya se me hizo tarde! ¡Alúcenme aquí! ¡No sean güeyes! Fuímonos al* night-night!

(To his COUSIN)

'¡Hora sí, Primo! Goodnight *porque ya se va metiendo la luna. ¡A dormir se ha dicho!*

VIEJO CAPULET

Como dice el dicho: Old *cholos* never die. They just go to sleep, *Carnal. Ahí nos watchamos,* Homes.

CAPULET

You said it, Homes. Buenas noches!

(Everyone except JULIET and *LA* NURSE begins to exit.)

JULIET

¡*Eit*! Psst! ¡*Ven pa'aca!* ¿*Quién es ese vato firme?*

NURSE

¡*Ese es el hijo de Tiburcio, el que tiene friegos de feria!*

JULIET

No, ¿*quién es el que se va saliendo 'horita?* The one that's leaving, ¿Ey?

NURSE

Pos ése se me hace que es aquel pachuco El Flaco.

JULIET

¡*Nombre, esta* chick!! ¡*Te sales!* ¡*Yo digo el que sigue de él!* The one that *no quiso* dance!

NURSE

¿*Pos quién sabe Tú?*

JULIET

¡*Con una chin . . .* ! Go and ask! ¡*'Juesú!*

(*Se va LA* NURSE chick *a preguntar.*)

¡*Si está casado mejor muero en vez de casarme con un baboso!*

NURSE

(Returning.)

Se llama por nombre Romeo. Pero ése cabrón es un Montesco y es el único hijo de tu peor enemigo.

JULIET

(Talking to herself, *la* chick.)

¡A la fregada! ¡No lo puedo creer! ¡El único hombre que amo es el hijo del mismo diablo que odio! Lo vi demasiado temprano sin conocerlo, and now it's too late. *Qué babosada la mía. El amor qué enamora al enemigo es amor qué enamora sin sentido.*

NURSE

¡Ay, Dios mío! ¿Qué es lo que dices?

JULIET

Nombre no es nada más que un poemita que me enseño este dude *que* danced *conmigo.*

(Someone *del otro lado* calls, "Juliet!")

NURSE

¡Ya vamos, pues! ¡Vente, mi 'ja! All the *vatos locos ya se fueron.*

(They exit, *y se acabó el pedo*—for now.)

(END OF SCENE)

QUESTIONS

1. What liberties does the playwright take in adapting Shakespeare's original scene?
2. What is the value of introducing bilingualism or multilingualism in the classroom or for public performance?
3. The author's book description states that he uses code-switching in part to entertain and in part to challenge his boundaries as a writer, to stretch his vocal chords, so to speak, but also in part to challenge the lingering prejudice against such mestizaje--or meeting and mixing of cultures (and also voices)--and help convert our society into one that accepts itself as it is: polyglossic and stronger for it." How does this adapted scene help accomplish the author's stated purpose?
4. What is empowering about this adapted scene?

WRITING PROMPTS

1. Reimagine a new ending to a book or play or film. Write it?
2. Reimagine a scene from a book, play, or film. Write it.

About The Author

Daniel García Ordaz is the founder of the Rio Grande Valley International Poetry Festival and the author of *You Know What I'm Sayin'?* His focus is on the power of language, which he celebrates in his writings and talks. He defended his thesis, *Cenzontle/Mockingbird: Empowerment Through Mimicry*, to complete his terminal degree, an MFA in Creative Writing from The University of Texas-Rio Grande Valley and he has edited and co-edited several books.

García is a teacher at La Joya Early College High School, a writer, and a recognized voice in Mexican American poetry. His work has appeared in numerous literary journals, academic collections, and anthologies. He was born in Houston in 1971 and raised in Mission, Texas. His publishing experience including editing and book cover design credits.

García also a song-writer, former newspaper journalist, photographicationisticator, and word-maker-upper. He appears in the documentary, "ALTAR: Cruzando fronteras/Building bridges" itself an altar offering to the late Chicana scholar and artist Gloria E. Anzaldúa, one of his great influences for this collection. García was one of five authors and the only poet chosen to participate in the Texas Latino Voices project in 2009 by the Texas Center For The Book, the state affiliate of the Library of Congress. He has been a featured reader and guest at numerous literary events, including the Texas Book Festival, Dallas International Book Fair, McAllen Book Festival, Texas Library Association events, TAIR, TABE, and Border Book Bash, among others.

García also served in the U.S. Navy as a Hospital Corpsman. He earned his Bachelor of Arts degree in English from The University of Texas-Pan American. He lives in the Rio Grande

Valley of deep South Texas with his wife, Gina, and their children and he continues to teach write, sing, and spend time in front of a crowd as often as he can. See videos of him on youtube and follow him at @poetmariachi.

Also by
Daniel García Ordaz

You Know What I'm Sayin'?
*(Poetry*Drama)*
ISBN-10: 0978995414

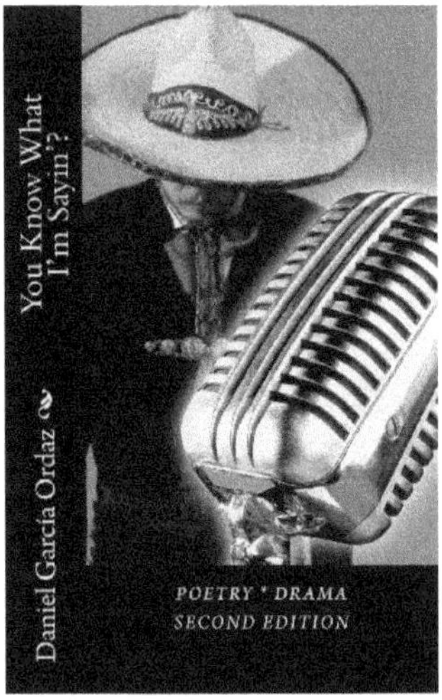

Cenzontle/Mockingbird:
Songs of Empowerment
*(Poetry*Drama)*
ISBN-10: 0692077529

www.ingramcontent.com/pod-product-compliance
Lightning Source LLC
Chambersburg PA
CBHW032145040426
42449CB00005B/407
9781732810600